THE EDWARDIAN LADY

The EDWARDIAN LADY

BIRTHDAY BOOK

Published by Henry Holt and Company, Inc.,
115 West 18th Street, New York, New York 10011.

Design © 1992 by Tigerprint Limited

The Country Diary of an Edwardian Lady
was published by Michael Joseph/Webb & Bower in 1977.
Copyright © 1977 by Richard Webb Ltd.

Printed in Hong Kong

ISBN 0-8050-2547-2

1   3   5   7   9   10   8   6   4   2

Water Hen
or
Moor Hen.

JANUARY

1

2

3

4

The Yew (Taxus baccata)

# JANUARY

_____ 5 _____

_____ 6 _____

_____ 7 _____

A wet January
A wet spring'.

JANUARY

8

9

10

11

JANUARY

12

13

14

Daisy
(Bellis perennis)

 # JANUARY

15

16

17

JANUARY

18

19

20

21

JANUARY

22

23

24

Cole Tit
Great Tit

JANUARY

---------- 25 ----------

---------- 26 ----------

---------- 27 ----------

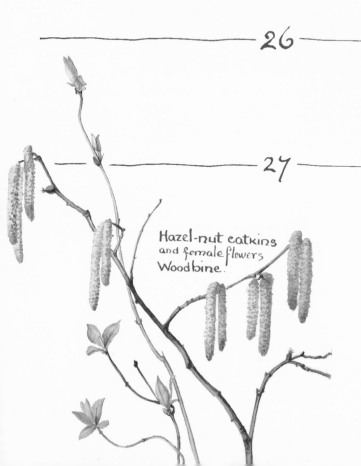

Hazel-nut catkins
and female flowers
Woodbine.

JANUARY

28

29

30

31

Common
Gorse
or
Whin
(Ulex Europæus)

Catkins of Aspen (Populus trémula)

FEBRUARY

——————————— *1* ———————————

——————————— *2* ———————————

——————————— *3* ———————————

——————————— *4* ———————————

Fair Maids
of
February

FEBRUARY

———————————— *5* ————————————

———————————— *6* ————————————

———————————— *7* ————————————

———————————— *8* ————————————

Unfolding leaves
of
Wild Arum
or Cuckoo Pint

FEBRUARY

9

10

The Erd Shrew or Shrew Mouse

 FEBRUARY

_____ 11 _____

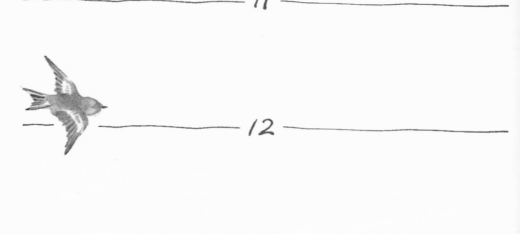

_____ 12 _____

_____ 13 _____

_____ 14 _____

 FEBRUARY

15

16

FEBRUARY

_____ 17 _____

_____ 18 _____

_____ 19 _____

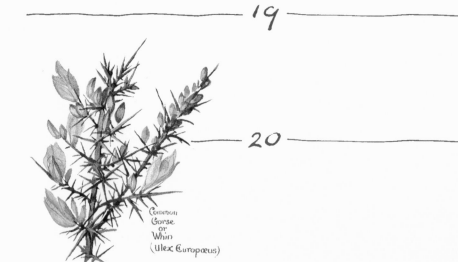

_____ 20 _____

Common
Gorse
or
Whin
(Ulex Europæus)

21

22

23

Goat Willow or Round-leaved Sallow
(Salix caprea)
Purple Willow (Salix purpures)
and
Alder (Alnus glutinosa)

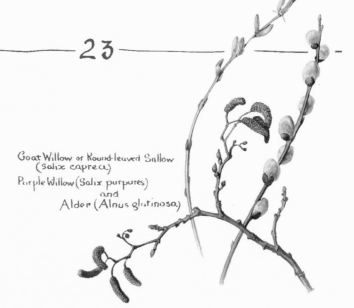

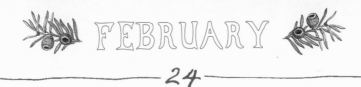

FEBRUARY

_____ 24 _____

_____ 25 _____

_____ 26 _____

_____ 27 _____

DANIEL DOOGAN HAY _28_

_29_

Picked some Dog's Mercury in flower,
This is the first to blossom of
all the wild herbaceous plants,
Daisies and Groundsel excepted

'Daffodils, that come before the swallow dares, And take the winds of March with beauty.' Shakespere.

Violets dim, yet sweeter than the lids of Juno's eyes or Cytherea's breathe. Shakespere. Winter's Tale

Sweet Violet (Viola odorata)

MARCH

1

2

TIMOTHY ARTHUR MARTIN
3

4

Then the thrushes sang
And shook my pulses and the elm's new leaves.' of Blackbird.
E.B.Browning.

Nest and eggs

MARCH

Wren

---------------- 5 ----------------

---------------- 6 ----------------

---------------- 7 ----------------

House Sparrow
Starling

MARCH

8

9

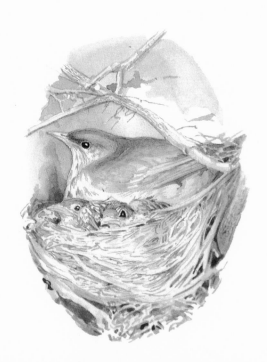

MARCH

Wood Moschatel
(Adoxa moschatel)

----- 10 -----

----- 11 -----

----- 12 -----

MARCH

13

SUE McKINLEY 14

MARCH

15

16

17

Chaffinch

Blue & White Periwinkle (Vinca minor)

MARCH

_____ 18 _____

_____ 19 _____

_____ 20 _____

_____ 21 _____

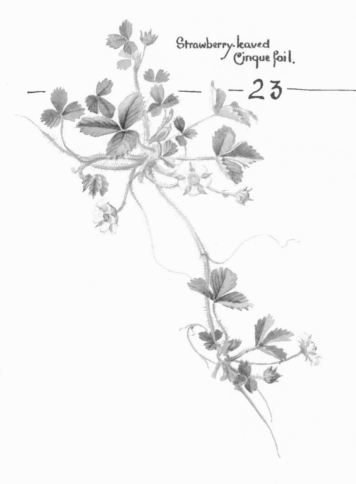

Strawberry-leaved
Cinque foil.

MARCH

TERASA MARTIN ——— 24 ———————————————

——————————————— 25 ———————————————

——————————————— 26 ———————————————

Song Thrush   Missel Thrush
        Hedge Sparrow

MARCH

27

CALEB MARTIN 28

JULIE MARTIN 29

30

MARCH

31

Wild Pear (*Pyrus Communis*)

Germander Speedwell
(*Veronica chamædris*)

Wood Anemone or Wind·flower
Anemone nembrosa
Dog Violet (*Viola canina*)

Primrose
(*Primula vulgaris*)

APRIL

1

2

3

4

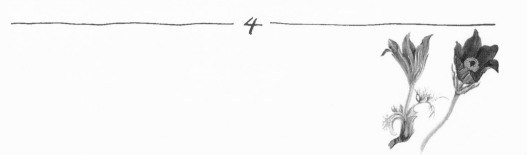

APRIL

_____ 5 _____

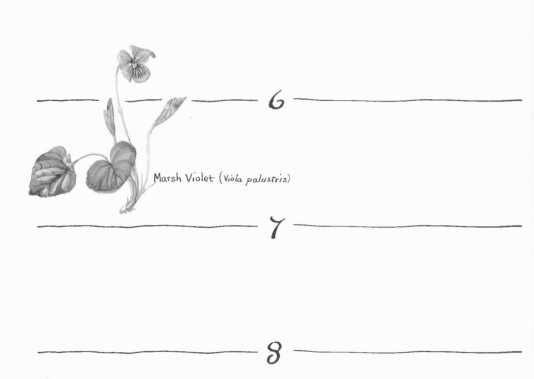

_____ 6 _____

Marsh Violet (_Viola palustris_)

_____ 7 _____

_____ 8 _____

APRIL

_____ 9 _____

_____ 10 _____

_____ 11 _____

Marsh Marigold
or Ranunculous
(Caltha palustris)

APRIL

———————— 12 ————————

———————— 13 ————————

———————— 14 ————————

———————— 15 ————————

16

17

Evergreen Alkanet
(Anchusa sempervirens)

Brimstone Butterfly
(Gonepteryx Rhamni)

Ground Ivy (Nepeta glechoma.)

APRIL

_18_ _____

_19_ _____

_20_ _____

_21_ _____

APRIL

22

23

24

APRIL

————————— 25 —————————

————————— 26 —————————

————————— 27 —————————

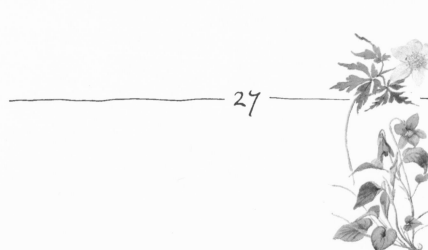

APRIL

28

29

30

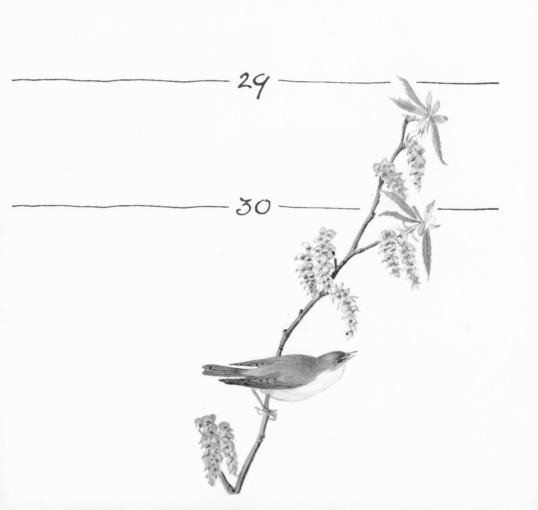

Chaffinch's nest
and eggs.
Hawthorn blossom and Wild Hyacinths.

 MAY

1

2

3

4

Common Broom
(Sarothamnus scoparius)

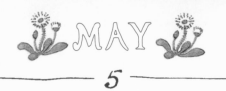

MAY

5

6

7

8

9

10

And after April
When May follows
And the white-throat builds
And all the swallows.'
R.B.

MAY

11

12

13

14

MAY

15

16

17

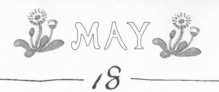

MAY

_____ 18 _____

_____ 19 _____

_____ 20 _____

Oak-blossom
and Oak-apple
(*Quercus robur*)

MAY

21

22

Blossom of Holly

23

24

 **MAY**

25

26

27

Blossom of Maple

MAY

28

29

30

31

Fox-glove (*Digitalis purpurea*)
Trailing Rose (*Rosa arvensis*)

JUNE

_____ *1* _____

_____ *2* _____

_____ *3* _____

_____ *4* _____

Yellow Iris or Flag
(*Iris Pseud-acoris*)

Demoiselle Dragon-fly (female)
(*Calopteryx splendens*)

JUNE

_____ 7 _____

_____ 8 _____

_____ 9 _____

_____ 10 _____

 JUNE

Orange-tip Butterfly
(Euchloe Cardimines)

———————————————— 11 ————————————————

———————————————— 12 ————————————————

———————————————— 13 ————————————————

JUNE

―――――――――― 14 ――――――――――

―――――――――― 15 ――――――――――

" June damp and warm Does the farmer no harm"

JUNE

─────────── 16 ───────────

─────────── 17 ───────────

Wild Service Tree
(Pyrus terminalis)

JUNE

_18_

_19_

_20_

JUNE

21

22

23

 # JUNE

24

25

JUNE

Water For-get-me-not.
Myosotis palustris

26

27

JUNE

28

29

30

Than the green rushes—O so glossy green,
The rushes they would whisper, rustle, shake,
And forth on floating gauze, no jewelled queen,
So rich, the green-eyed dragon-flies would break
And hover on the flowers – aerial things;
With little rainbows flickering on their wings'.
                                        Jean Ingelow.

Great Burnet
(sanguisorba officinalis)

Beaked Sedge und Common Rush.   Ragged Robin (Lychnis flos-cuculi)

JULY

——————————— *1* ———————————

——————————— *2* ———————————

——————————— *3* ———————————
Magpie Moth

——————————— *4* ———————————

Common Ragwort
(Senicis jacobaea)

JULY

5

6

7

8

JULY

——— 9 ———

——— 10 ———

——— 11 ———

Meadow
Crane's-bill
(Geranium pratense)

JULY

_12_

_13_

"In July shear your rye."

_14_

_15_

JULY

ERIN MARTIN ———— **16** ————————————————

———————————— **17** ————————————————

———————————— **18** ————————————————

Branched Bur Reed (Sparganium ramosum)   Spotted Palmate Orchis (Orchis maculata)
Common Flowering Rush (Butomus umbellatus)   Rosebay Willow-Herb (Epilobium angustifolium)

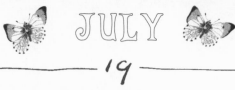

JULY

19

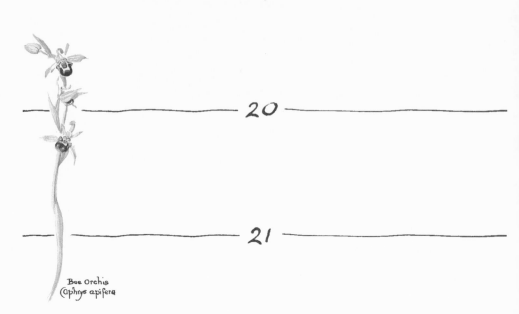

20

21

Bee Orchis
Ophrys apifera

22

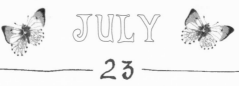 JULY

23

24

25

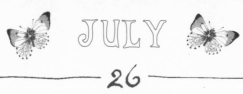

JULY

———————— 26 ————————

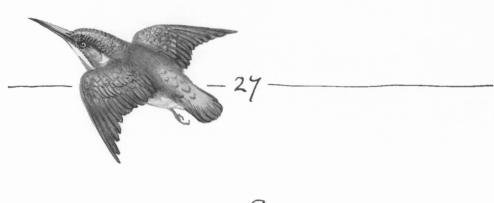

———————— 27 ————————

———————— 28 ————————

———————— 29 ————————

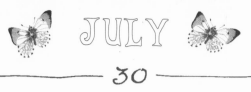

JULY

30

31

AUGUST

_____ 1 _____

_____ 2 _____

_____ 3 _____

Creeping Loose-strife

_____ 4 _____

AUGUST

--- 5 ---

--- 6 ---

--- 7 ---

JOSEPH BRADFORH 8 MARTIN

Heather or Ling
(Calluna vulgaris)

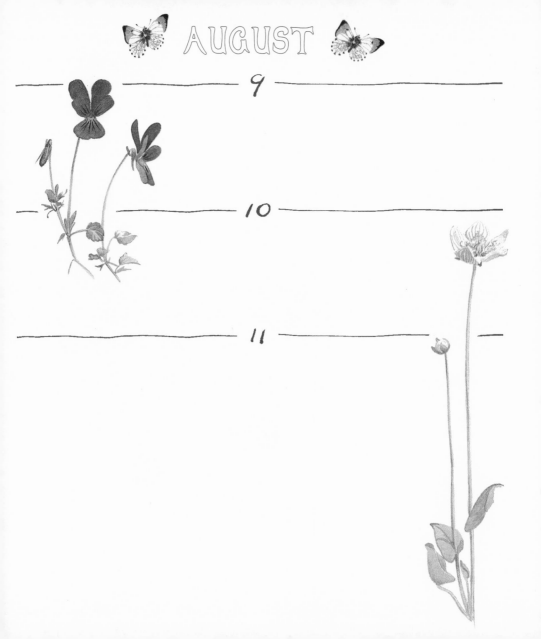

AUGUST

9

10

11

AUGUST

—————————————— 12 ——————————————

—————————————— 13 ——————————————

—————————————— 14 ——————————————

Common Red Poppy
(*Papaver Rhaeas*)

Hare-bell
(*Campanula rotundifolia*)

Mayweed
(*Matricaria moderata*)

AUGUST

15

16

17

Cross-leaved Heath
(Erica Tetralix)

18

AUGUST

19 ——————

20 ——————

Creeping Plume Thistle
(Cnicus arvensis)

21 ——————

Cotton Thistle.
(Onopordum acanthium)

AUGUST

22

23

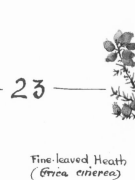

Fine-leaved Heath
(*Erica cinerea*)

24

25

 # AUGUST

---- 26 ----

---- 27 ----

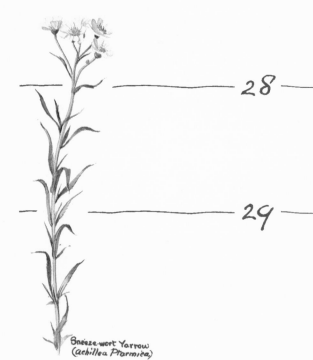

---- 28 ----

---- 29 ----

Sneeze-wort Yarrow
(Achillea Ptarmica)

AUGUST

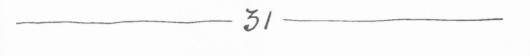

30

31

Fruit
of Spanish Chesnut (Castanea vesca)
and
Horse Chesnut (Œsculus Hippocastanum)

Goldfinch
feeding on
Thistle-seed.

 SEPTEMBER

1

2

3

4

Juniper berries
(Juniperus communis)

SEPTEMBER

_____ 5 _____

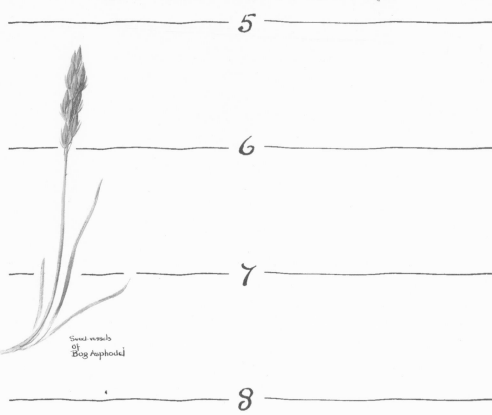

_____ 6 _____

_____ 7 _____

Seed-vessels
of
Bog Asphodel

_____ 8 _____

SEPTEMBER

9

10

11

SEPTEMBER

12

13

14

15

Round-leaved Sundew
(Drosera rotundifolia)

SEPTEMBER

_____ 16 _____

_____ 17 _____

_____ 18 _____

Fruit
of
Wild Guelder Rose
(Viburnum opulus)

SEPTEMBER

19

20

House Sparrows
and
Oats.

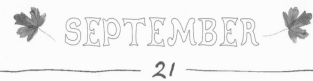

SEPTEMBER

21

22

23

24

SEPTEMBER

25

26

Goldfinch
feeding on
Thistle-seed

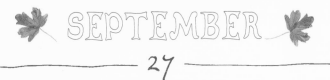

SEPTEMBER

27

28

29

30

Yellow-Hammers
feeding in stubble

OCTOBER

1

2

3

4

Fruit
of
Wild Service Tree
(Pirus torminalis)

OCTOBER

5

6

Under a dark, red-fruited
yew-tree's shade!
M. Arnold.

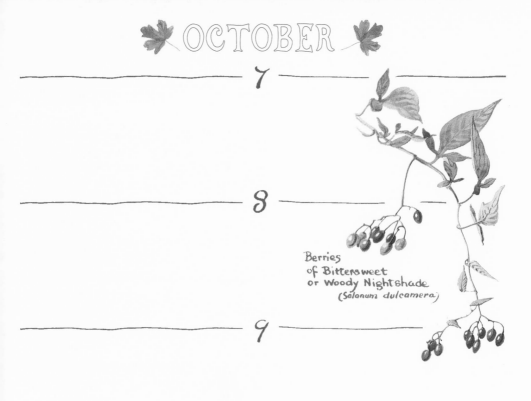

OCTOBER

7

8

Berries
of Bittersweet
or Woody Nightshade
(Solanum dulcamera)

9

10

OCTOBER

———— 11 ————

———— 12 ————

———— 13 ————

———— 14 ————

OCTOBER

———————————————— *15* ————————————

———————————————— *16* ————————————

———————————————— *17* ————————————

 OCTOBER

18

19

20

OCTOBER

————————— 21 —————————

————————— 22 —————————

————————— 23 —————————

————————— 24 —

Beech
(*Fagus sylvatica*)

OCTOBER

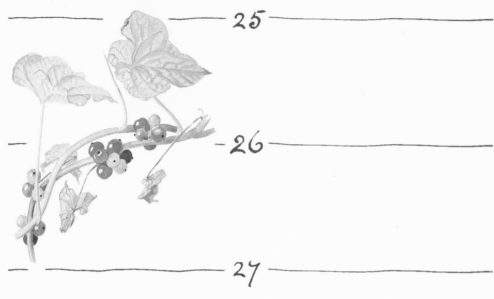

25

26

27

28

OCTOBER

29

30

31

Fruit
of Elder-berry tree
(Sambucus nigra)

Leaves of Sycamore (*Acer pseudo platanus*)
and Small Maple (*Acer pseudo campestris*)

NOVEMBER

_____ 1 _____

_____ 2 _____

_____ 3 _____

_____ 4 _____

Toad-stools

NOVEMBER

5

6

7

8

 # NOVEMBER

9 ——————

10 ——————

11 ——————

Starling
(Sturnus vulgaris)

NOVEMBER

12

13

14

Bramble leaves

NOVEMBER

15

16

17

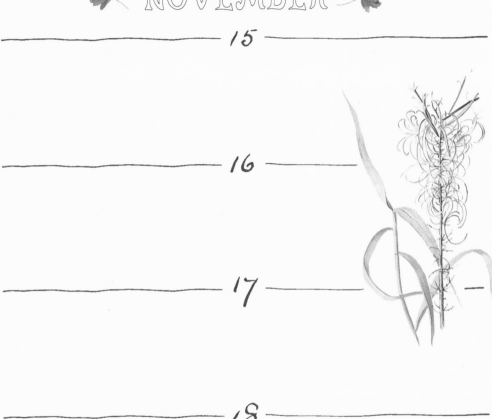

18

NOVEMBER

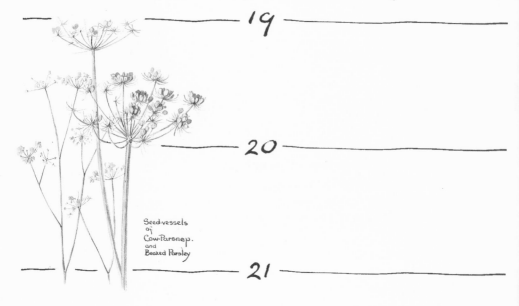

Seed-vessels
of
Cow-Parsnep.
and
Beaked Parsley

19

20

21

22

NOVEMBER

23

24

25

The Sulphur-tuft
(agaricus fascicularis)

Common
Polyporus
(Polyporus versicolor)

Stag's Horn
Fungi.

NOVEMBER

--- 26 ---

--- 27 ---

--- 28 ---

--- 29 ---

Green Woodpecker
(Gecinus viridis)

Nipple-wort
and
Dock

It's verdure trails
the Ivy shoot
Along the ground
from root to root ;
Or climbing high
With random maze,
O'er elm, and ash and alder strays,
And round each trunk
a net-work weaves,
Fantastic, and each bough with leaves
Of countless shapes, entwines and studs
With pale green blooms
and half formed buds.
The Ivy, of our native flowers
That now among the latest pours
It's pale green bloom, and ripes it's seed
Of black and shining balls to feed,
Impervious to the winter's frost,
The little bird's afflicted host;
The Ivy, fairest plant to seize
And promptest on the neighbouring trees
O'er bole and branch with leaves that shine
All glossy bright, tenacious twine
And the else naked woodland scene
Clothe with a raiment
Fresh and green.'
                            Bishop Mant

Common Ivy
(Hedera Hélix)

# DECEMBER

1

2

3

4

 DECEMBER

JOE McKINLEY _____ 5 _____

_____ 6 _____

_____ 7 _____

_____ 8 _____

Mistletoe
(Viscus album

DECEMBER

9

10

11

DECEMBER

———— 12 ————

———— 13 ————

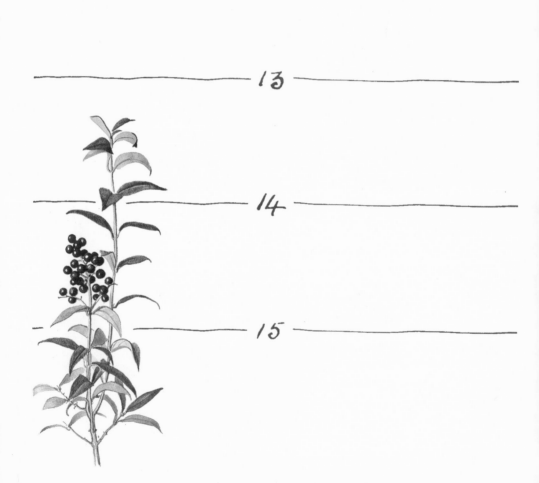

———— 14 ————

———— 15 ————

 DECEMBER

_____ 16 _____

ELAINE MARTIN HAY 17 _____

_____ 18 _____

DECEMBER

19

20

21

Holly (Ilex aquifolium)

22

MCLAIN MARTIN   23

24

25

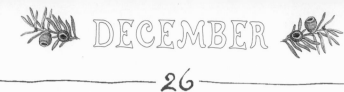# DECEMBER

26

27

28

29

DECEMBER

30

31